# Lorri Bach

# Middle

# Update

The life and times of a middle school teacher

© 2019 - Lorri Bach

**Lorri Bach**
**Middle School Update**
All rights reserved. No part of this publication may be reproduced, stored in a retrieval system or transmitted in any form or by any means, electronic, mechanical, photocopying, recording or otherwise without the prior permission of the publisher or in accordance with the provisions of the Copyright, Designs and Patents Act 1988 or under the terms of any licence permitting limited copying issued by the Copyright Licensing Agency.

**Published by: P&B Publishing;** Chris Russell/Lorri Bach

**Page Layout/Graphics/Art Design by: P&B Publishing;**
Chris Russell, Columbus, Georgia

**Cover Design by: P&B Publishing;**
Chris Russell, Columbus, Georgia

A CIP record for this book is available from the Library of Congress Cataloging-in-Publication Data

**IISBN-13:** 978-1-7338923-1-5

**Distributed by:** Ingram Spark

# Middle School Update
## LORRI BACH

*The life and times of a middle school teacher*

# Dedication

Above all, I dedicate this book to Jesus Christ. I am incredibly grateful for His unconditional love, and the knowledge that I am covered by grace, regardless of circumstances. To be a Christ-follower is the greatest blessing I can imagine.

"For I know the plans I have for you," says the Lord, "plans to prosper you, to give you hope and a future."
(Jeremiah 29:11)

**To my mom**, Joy Bach: Mom, you are an amazing, remarkable woman. Thank you for being an inspiration not only to me, but to others as well. You make a positive difference in the lives of everyone who is blessed to know you. Thank you for setting a positive example for me to follow. I am so grateful to have a mom who demonstrates kindness and compassion to others. Thank you for your support, encouragement, and unconditional love. Although many miles separate us, you are always there for me. Thank you for lifting me up to the Lord every day in your prayers. Regardless of the challenges you face, your faith never wavers. Even now, as you learn to accept a future without dad, you are truly an example of unwavering steadfastness and strength. Thank you for the gift of you. I am incredibly thankful to be your daughter. I love you more than I can express in words.

***To my dad***, John Bach: As I write this, I am overwhelmed with thankfulness for the blessing of being your daughter. Today would have been your birthday, and I can't think of a more appropriate gift than to dedicate this book to you. It was your dream as well as mine that this book would someday be published, and I know that you are celebrating in heaven. Dad, thank you for valuing the time we spent together. I am blessed with unforgettable memories. Thank you for loving my mom. Thank you for taking time to listen. Thank you for believing in me. I am grateful for a dad who authentically lived his faith, and trusted the Lord for guidance and wisdom. I am incredibly thankful for you. Thank you for choosing to be my dad. I love you.

**To my students**, past and present: I am grateful to have an opportunity to be a teacher. People often tell me that my students are lucky to be in my class, but the truth is that I am the lucky one. My students are a blessing. Thank you for providing the material for this book! You might recognize your contributions within the pages. It is my hope that I have made a positive difference in your lives.

Publishing this book is the fulfillment of a dream that has been embedded in my heart for decades. My heart is full of thankfulness.

Lorri Bach
July 3, 2019

## Introduction

When Lorri was still in the crawling stage, I knew I was dealing with a strong-willed child.

If she crawled into a wall, she kept rocking against it, waiting for it to move. I would pick her up, turn her around and off she would go. As she grew older, she kept me on my toes. I needed to be very aware of my words or they would come back to haunt me. I could tell her, "I never want to see you doing that again." She would then do it in the other room. When I called her on it, she would say, "You didn't see me doing it again."

Now she's dealing with students like that all day. She's the perfect teacher for them. She knows their tricks and she loves them. They are like her children. She attends their concerts and sports events. She makes each school day special. Just as a good parent would, every child in Lorri's classroom receives individual attention from her.

Even after they are no longer her students, she keeps in touch with them and they keep in touch with her. No longer the tricksters, they tell her of their weddings and births of their babies.

When she would visit me and her dad, she would tell us stories about her "children."

Even though her dad is no longer with us, one of his last desires was that this book get published.

As her parents we are so very proud of her.

Joy Bach

Welcome to Ms. Bach's Lovely Classroom!

Chapter 1:

# Context Clues

*Does drawing conclusions require crayons and colored pencils?*

Me: "Hey, I got an awesome penguin keychain!"
Student: "Uh, Ms. Bach, that's an owl."
Me: "Oh."
Awkward silence.
Me: "Hey, I got an awesome owl keychain!"

As an entry task, I asked students to write a statement and then make an inference about the statement.
Statement: "I have fifteen brothers and sisters."
Inference: "My dad needs to get a new hobby."

Students were asked to write a paragraph about a non-fiction topic and then make an inference about one of the stated facts.

Statement: "The male African Lion has the ability to have sex up to seventy times a day."

Inference: "If you see a lion at the zoo and he is just lying there, he is probably just really tired."

Good inference, kid! Closing the achievement gap, one student at a time!

My class planned to go on a field trip to the woods to study forestry, wildlife, soil, water, and outdoor recreation. After discussing the field trip schedule, one student raised his hand and asked, "Do we have to wear pants?"

After analyzing and reviewing a scoring rubric used to determine writing proficiency, the students were given an opportunity to score released anchor papers previously submitted by students.

As we discussed the official scores for each writing sample based on the domains of the scoring rubric, one student was surprised when a paper received a score of two (out of five) for ideas.

"Why did this paper get a two?" he asked. "It had a lot of supporting details and information!"

After explaining to the student that the information in the paper was inaccurate, since Velcro wasn't actually grown on farms, the student said, "Oh yeah! It's grown in vineyards!"

While discussing the school talent show, one student asked:

"What language was the Russian song in?"

On Friday the 13th, I wrote the word superstitious on the board and discussed its meaning with the students.

Student: "Where did you find that word?"

Me: "In the dictionary."

Student: "Which one?"

Me: "The one on the shelf."

Later in the class period, I was summoned to the desk of the student who had previously asked the question about the word.

Pointing to his laptop screen, he said, "I've looked everywhere and can't find the word!" I wasn't surprised. He was searching for "the shelf" online. Imagine his awe and wonder when I directed him to an actual bookshelf and handed him a dictionary. It was a life-changing moment!

"When is the Friday Field Trip?"

Chapter 2:
# Memorable Quotes

*I would caution my students to think before they speak, but they would probably ask me what I wanted them to think about!*

"My favorite class is band because I love to play the tub."

"He was a convicted felon. That wasn't good."

"My favorite animal is the Cheeto."

"My pockets don't have pants!"

"Everyone over the age of thirty is older than all the dogs in the world."

"My birthday is in January on the 6th. I'm going to Chunk E. Cheese!"

"It's not lost. I just can't find it!"

"Say no to drugs, but say yes to tacos."

"I was accidentally talking!"

**"Instead of coming to school, can you just come to my house to teach me? I'll make you waffles!"**

"Ms. Bach, tell us one of your stories that make us laugh so hard that tears come out our eyes."

"Can you explain that again? To be honest with you, I was off in La La Land."

"This class is the best part of my day!"

"I don't understand proposition phrases!"

"How do you spell that in cursive?"

"I can help if someone is choking because I know the Heimlich Remover!"

"I made you a cookie, but I ate it. I guess it's the thought that counts!"

"Wow, Ms. Bach, what happened? You look really nice today! Are you going on a date or something?"

My students worked on a project, creating and writing their own books with hard covers and hand-stitched bindings. One student included a copyright page which stated: "If you copy my book, Santa will put you on the naughty list!"

"Sometimes I'm confused out loud!"

CHAPTER 3:

# Vocabulary Variations

*Though humorous, my hope is that my students will realize the importance of proofreading as an essential component of the writing process. Have people really been to constipation camps?*

The students completed a vocabulary pre-assessment for words they would encounter in a story, and came up with some interesting interpretations:
1) SUBDUED: When the substitute teacher gives you an assignment and it is due
2) OMINOUS: When you write something but don't use your real name
3) OVATION: A word women use when they are trying to get pregnant
4) REVERENCE: When your church has more than one pastor

Dear Student,

When you are writing an essay in which you attempt to encourage people to participate in the election process, you might want to consider changing the spelling of the word election.

There isn't an "r" in the word, so you should change the "r" to an "l" prior to submitting your essay.

Thank you,
Ms. Bach

Machinery (a student's definition):
"Someone who goes to other countries to tell people about God."

During first period, I talked to the students about the kind of morning I was having, including the part about hitting a raccoon with my car while I drove to work. Later in the class period as they were completing a writing assignment, a student asked how to spell the word "dying."

Before I could say anything, another student said "R-A-C-C-O-O-N."

Question: Where in each story can you find information about new and challenging words?
Response: "I don't know. Probably in the glossionary."
Is that a glossary/dictionary hybrid?

"While I was at the fair, I got on the Sister."
I really hope that the "Sister" is a ride at the fair.

While writing a poem about themselves, one student wrote that she was "afraid of snacks." I wondered which snacks frightened her the most.

Twinkies? Gummy Bears? Chocolate Covered Peanuts? Potato Chips?

Question: What is something you have enjoyed so far this school year?
Response: "I have enjoyed melting new friends!"
That is certainly an unusual talent.

Question: What is something that annoys you?
Response: "What bugs me is sprinkles. They go dink, dink, dink, dink, dink. Over and over."
Was he talking about sprinklers?

"My favorite video game is Modern *Warefare* 3"
Modern *Warefare?* Seriously?
There is a video game about kitchen utensils? Who knew?

Do you fight with spatulas, rolling pins, and whisks? Do you drive a grill instead of a tank?

Do you get bonus points for creating the best dinner party?

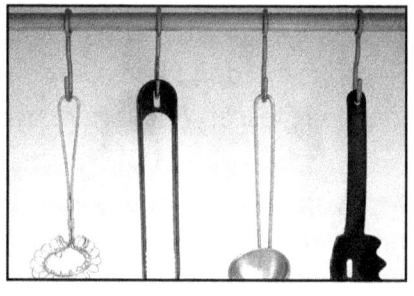

## From a student poem titled, *My Favorite Sport*

"My favorite sport is bassball. I love to play bassball with my "*farter.*" When I hit the ball, I run around the basses, and sometimes I slide home."
Does he use a fishing pole as a bat?

"Ms. Bach, I couldn't finish my homework because I had to stay with my uncle while my parents went to a marriage retreatment."

"I need to improve my writing. My sentences need more comas and atrophies."

Will I go to sleep if I read them? I hope she meant commas and apostrophes.

"Did you know that there were over 100 pyramids in an Egyptian dessert?"

What dessert was it? Pharoah's Pie? King Tut Cookies?

Although students at my school wear uniforms, we have been discussing an option that would allow them to wear jeans on Fridays. I asked the class to write about their opinion on the subject, and explain the reasons why this change in the dress code should or should not be implemented.

One student wrote: "We should get to wear jeans because we are tired of wearing cakes!"

Yeah, kid, I wouldn't want to wear cakes to school either! Oh, did you mean KHAKIS?

Question: What is your favorite food?
Response: "I love chessburgers!"
I might be confused, but I thought chess was a board game.

In my class, students have opportunities to learn about word usage and vocabulary, as well as the essential elements of effective oral presentations.

Therefore, in preparation for our Dead Word Funeral, the students created colorful tombstones for the words that should be eliminated from their writing. They wrote eulogies which described the origin of the word, explained ways in which the word was overused, and offered condolences to the surviving "synonym" family members.

When I asked the students to submit their tombstones, one boy said, "Mine is almost done. I am still working on the urology."

Question: What is your favorite animal?
Response: "My favorite animal is the Bagel Tiger."

Question: What is your favorite mode of writing?
Response: "The pervasive essay."

Question: What is your favorite mode of writing?
Response: "I like writing for different porpoises."

Question: Why does every complete sentence need a subject and a predicate?
Response: "Every sentence needs a subject and a pedicure because it just wouldn't be complete without it."

Question: What is your favorite snack?
Response: "My favorite snack is Peanut Butter and Quakers."

Question: What do you think the word harried means?
Response: "Isn't it like Chewbacca?"

## *Free Write Friday and Bad Mitten?*

"My favorite game is Bad Mitten. Have you ever played Bad Mitten, Ms. Bach?"

My students had been writing persuasive essays.

One student wrote: "Teachers should have more celery because they need it to do their jobs." I hope he meant "salary." It would be a little weird if he had some insight in regard to our need for dietary fiber.

"Ms. Bach, what should I write in the table of continents?"
You could start with Asia.

"Ms. Bach, can I please move to another seat? He keeps destructing me!"
Well, of course you can move to another seat! No child will be destructed in my class!
Good grief, the nonsense that goes on around here.

After explaining to the students that all words serve a purpose, I pointed to an "a" within the context of a sentence and asked them what it was.
Student A: "It's a letter."
Me: "Of course it's a letter, but what purpose does it serve within the sentence?"
Student A: "It's a vowel!"
At this point, another student offered assistance. "I know what it is! It's a particle!"

At least it RHYMED with article.

"Ms. Bach, did you used to watch the Ducks of Hazzard?"

"The man couldn't prance the words because he was from another country."

I haven't seen anyone "prance" words before, but it could be interesting!

A student used the word "inspontaneously" during a presentation.

Apparently, it meant that something happened instantly and spontaneously at the same time. It's an adverb hybrid!

The students wrote about the best birthday gifts they ever received. A few highlights:
1) A skate broad
2) A paint set, which was his favorite because he wants to be an artist like Pablo Pistachio
3) A pet snack

Aw, c'mon. Get the kid a real pet. How can he take his Twinkie or his Gummy Bear for a walk?

My students took a quiz on idioms that we have studied this year.

Here are some of my favorite responses:
"Feather in Your Cat" (Feather in Your Cap)
"It's Raining Small Domesticated Animals" (It's Raining Cats and Dogs)
"Cat Got Your Thong?" (Cat Got Your Tongue)
"Apple in Your Pie" (Apple of Your Eye)

Student: "Ms. Bach, I licked a glue stick."
Me: "Why would you do something like that?"
Student: "Someone double-dog dared me."
Me: "How did that work out for you?"
Student: "Not so good. I should have held out for a triple-dog dare."

Student: "Ms. Bach, do you want a piece of gum?"
Me: "No thank you."
Student: "Are you sure? I sucked all the sugar off it already!"

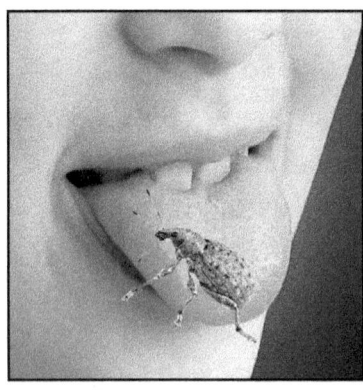

"My taste bugs love chocolate!"

"Taste bugs," I asked?

"What do you feed your taste bugs?"

CHAPTER 4:

# The Randomness of the Middle School Mind

*It is an understatement to say that the thoughts of a middle school student are random. Vocalizing whatever is on their mind is serious business. They are amazingly authentic.*

"The word root "therm" means "heat." Sort of like when I heat up something in the microwave. Thinking of that makes me hungry. I wish I had a taco."

"A Ulaaihawane is an extinct bird. Its name means "red bird that eats hawane" in Hawaiian. Don't ask me what the fudge a hawane is, because I don't know."

A group of boys were having a conversation in the hallway outside my classroom door. As I walked by, one of them said, "Ms. Bach, we were trying to help someone understand metaphors, so we were making comparisons between people and farm equipment. You were a tractor."

Should I be happy that they were helping someone understand metaphors, or concerned because I have been compared to a tractor?

Student: "What's your husband's name?"
Me: "I don't have a husband."
Student: "Really? You look like somebody who would have one."

Me: "Why are you drawing?"
Student: "I'm not drawing. I'm customizing the Fire Ninja suit."

Question: What can you do to make the world a better place?
Response: "Befriend a bear, inspire people, take showers, and eat more pie."

I reminded the students that there were only ten and a half school days left, but one student had a more impressive countdown statistic.
"Ms. Bach, in 3,218 days, I will be 21!"

In the Land of Boo, there are trees but no branches, floods but no rain, puppies but no dogs, queens but no kings, apples but no bananas, coffee but no tea, hugging but no dating, cookies but no cake, and basketball but no bowling.
Have you figured out the riddle for the Land of Boo? Welcome to my world!

Since the forecast called for snow, the students were talking about the possibility of a snow day.
Student: "Ms. Bach, we are having a snow day on Wednesday!"
Me: "How do you know that already? It isn't snowing yet."
Student: "It's snowing in my mind, Ms. Bach. It's snowing in my mind."

Question: What is the most practical use for duct tape? Response: "When a robber tries to steal from a store, the manager could duct tape him to the beef jerky aisle."

## *A Student's Insight Into The World*

"I will tell you my secret thoughts that will make you think I am crazy, so don't laugh. I think street signs should be pink, politicians should always tell the truth, there should be world peace, teachers shouldn't have a huge TV in the teacher's lounge, and TV shows shouldn't have commercials. Those are my secret thoughts."

During a discussion about the necessity of including details while describing a story character, the students were asked to draw a fictional character, and write a detailed description. One student wrote the following paragraph:

This is Billy Bob. He's a cowboy. You know he is a cowboy because he is wearing boots with those silver pointy things on the back. Billy Bob also has a big yee-haw hat. It's called a yee-haw hat because cowboys say "Yee-Haw!" I don't know what else cowboys say, because they mostly talk to their horses. He's not very tall, and has brown hair. PS: The spots on his boots are because he stepped in horse poop.

After the students read an article in a magazine about snack foods that contained synthetic flavor chemicals that made them taste good, they were asked to evaluate the article and share their opinions. One student wrote: "Give peas a chance!"

In all of my years of teaching middle school, I have never had a student bring a headless Barbie wearing tinfoil to my class. I didn't ask, I didn't even want to know. Epic.

Dear Ms. Bach,

I am sorry that I had a problem yesterday in class. I am having trouble processing my emotions because of puberty. I hope you understand.

Sincerely,
Michael

## *Describe the Qualities of a Good Leader*

Response: "A good leader should be short and have beautiful hair. They always wash their hands instead of using sanitizer, and they smell good most of the time."

I guess that about covers it.

## *Biography Research Report*

"Joe Montana had a girlfriend named Jennifer who was a model and actress. He proposed to her and she said yes. Now Joe is a normal person with a wife, and is too old to have a family. He is still alive, which is very important. Before he was old he played football in the NFL, and he was like the best player who was helpful to his team."

••••••••••••••••••••••••••••

We have been working on expository writing. One of the prompts asked students to write a descriptive paper about the dream house they would want to have:

"My dream house would have a basketball court, two swimming pools, a go-kart track, and a theater room where I could watch TV and play video games on a big screen. Next to the kitchen, I would have my own Starbucks. Anyone who comes to my house would have to know a password to get in the gate.

Sorry Ms. Bach, but you can't have the password. No teachers allowed. Well, unless you want to use my kitchen to bake some cookies."

Students were asked to write about their New Year's Resolution, describe the steps to achieve their goal, and explain why it is important.

Response: "My New Year's Resolution is to help my mom by working in the house. The steps I will take will be inside the house. This goal is important because it will keep me out of the yard where the dog poop is. I hope my dog makes a resolution not to poop."

We had a discussion about staying focused during class. I asked the students to create a list of possible distractions. One student's list: Darth Vader, bunnies, farting, singing, being bitten by a venomous spider, barfing, arm wrestling, and girls. As he was sharing his list, he said, "I don't mean you, Ms. Bach, I mean real girls."

I asked the students to write something they thought I should know about them. One student wrote: "You should know that I go off into an imaginary world sometimes, where I talk to monkeys. You can't talk to them because they are shy, and also because they are imaginary."

Sentence starter: If I were elected President of the United States, I would...

Response: "If I were elected President of the United States, I would make it illegal to be stupid. All stupid people would have to live in a place called Idiotopia. I've started a list of people who should go."

CHAPTER 5:

# The Joys of Teaching

*One of the greatest blessings of being a middle school teacher is the opportunity to have a career in which laughter and heartwarming moments occur often.*

A student attached a post-it note on an assignment and wrote this note:

"Please, Ms. Bach, please give me an A or a B or my mom will get uber mad at me. Trust me, she will lecture me for like ten hours. I'll be grounded from my room, so I will have to sleep on the couch where I will be closer to the lecturing."

Student: "Ms. Bach, you are my favorite teacher, and I want you to know that if you died, I would come to your funeral."
Me: "Would you stand up in front of everyone and say something?"
Student: "Sure, if anyone else showed up."
Thanks for the compliment and the ego boost, kid. I'd like to think that there might be a few people!

A student asked me how to spell the word "procrastination."
I told him I would tell him later.

## *Persuasive Writing*

Dear Aunt Mary,

How are you? Did you have a good Christmas? I was excited to have a break from school, but I wish we could have had snow, because I wanted to ride Cousin Bob's snowmobile.

I was hoping that I would be able to see you this summer at the family reunion, but mom says that you aren't coming. I remember what happened during the last family reunion, but I hope that I will be able to convince you to come back. It couldn't be that bad again, right?

One reason why you should come to the family reunion is that I promise to give you the correct address for our house this time. Who knew that mixing up a couple of numbers could cause so much trouble? Our neighbor is really sorry that he called the police when he found you in his house, the policeman is really sorry about the handcuffs and everything, the TV reporter is really sorry about filming you for the news, and we are really sorry about the misunderstanding. I learned a lesson about giving people accurate information, and our neighbor learned a lesson about keeping his door locked.

Another reason that you should come to the family reunion is that we have purchased a new terrarium for our pet snake Dexter, which has a locking lid. We are really sorry that you were scared when you found him in your bed when you woke up in the morning. Thank you for letting me sign your cast after you broke your foot trying to run out of the room.

Finally, I think that you should come because dad promises not to call you "Hairy Mary" anymore, even when he thinks you aren't listening. It's natural for a woman your age to have some facial hair, and we don't want to hurt your feelings. My friend's grandma has a longer beard than you, so you shouldn't worry about it.

I hope you will write back soon, and let me know your decision. It would be great to see you again!

Your nephew,
Lucas

......................................

Student: "Ms. Bach, does a Boise horse have babies?"
Me: "A Boise horse?"
Student: "Yeah, does a Boise horse have babies?"
Me: "What is a Boise horse?"
Student: "It's a seahorse that isn't a girl!"
I get it now! A boy seahorse!

## Birthday Stickers

As a continuation of my birthday celebration, some girls in my class gave me stickers with pictures of all the Disney Princesses. Being a good sport, I stuck them on my shirt for the rest of the day.

Guess who forgot to take the stickers off before having passport photos taken after school?

I have a job where these questions and statements actually make sense:
1. Don't lick the markers.
2. Why did you put a bean up your nose?
3. Thank you for the marshmallow sculpture.
4. No, I can't read Klingon. Please write using standard English.

..........................................

In response to a message written on the board reminding students that Teacher Appreciation Week was coming up, a student wrote that he would get me a $10 gift card to "Barns in Nobles." After that, someone drew a picture of a cow.

Student: "I can't turn in my project on Friday because I won't be here."
Me: "Turn it in Thursday."
Student: "I never thought of that! Thanks, Ms. Bach!"
Teachers are so full of life-changing wisdom.

> Don't give us too much homework. Your killing trees. ☹

I received a note from a student who said that she was going to give me a Christmas car! Sweet!

I wondered what kind of car it would be. Mustang? Acura? Lexus?

Student: "Ms. Bach, can I turn in my assignment on Friday?"
Me: "You don't have school on Friday because teachers will be preparing report cards." Student: "Can I bring it on Monday?"
Me: "There isn't school on Monday because of Columbus Day."
Student: "Well, when should I bring in my assignment?"
Me: "You could have turned it in when it was due."
Student: "Oh yeah, that makes sense."

Actual phrases used in class:
1. Don't lick the colored pencils.
2. It's not bunny poop. It's a chocolate-covered raisin.
3. Yes, I did wear this on purpose.
4. How old do you think I was when I was your age?

Write an end-of-the-year letter:
One student's response: "Ms. Bach, your letter is Q."
Technically, he DID follow directions.

Me: "Does anyone have any questions?"
Student "I don't have a question, but I just wanted to say that you did a good job today, Ms. Bach."

Me (while demonstrating a lesson): "Who is talking?"
Student: "You."
Brilliant.

## *Campfire Story Day* Reflections

1. Going into the woods is a bad idea.
2. Students watch too many horror movies and crime dramas.
3. I'm never going into a basement or attic again.
4. I might rethink my response in the future, when the students ask me if they can write scary stories. "How scary can they be?" is a question worthy of contemplative thought.

*Campfire Stories Today —Madyson*

    My students sat around fake campfires, held marshmallows on a stick, and shared stories they had written. Within the context of modern-day society, it sometimes seems as though storytelling has become a lost art. Many of the students have not listened to their parents or grandparents share stories during family gatherings. As I sat in their campfire circles, I was thankful for memories to share, and my own family of storytellers.

·······························

I totaled my car. When I told them their quizzes didn't survive the car accident, they begged me to let them do it again!

    Ha Ha! Yeah, right.

Dear Ms. Bach,

 I asked my mom to go to Starbucks on the way to school, because I remembered you said you like vanilla chai tea. Mom said we could go, so we went there and ordered one for you. I had never tried chai tea before, and it smelled so good that I didn't think you would mind if I tasted it. I'm sorry, but it was so good I drank the whole thing. You were right! It was good! At least I thought of you!

 Love,
 Erin

As I was cleaning my classroom, I found this note on my desk:

*You have made are seventh grade year so fun, extatic, and very hard-working*

"Dear Ms. Bach, I will miss you so much! You are an amazing teacher! You are the best teacher in the history of teaching!

Well, actually, my dad says that Jesus was the best teacher in history, so he has to be #1. I still love you the best at this school!"

Kid, your dad is right. Jesus should be #1!

Student: "Ms. Bach, I like your haircut!"
Me: "Thank you!"
Student: "I know other guys might not notice, but I am practicing these things so that I will be a good husband someday. If you hadn't gotten a haircut, I would have said something nice about your sweater."

While working on a book-making project, one of my students accidentally chopped off a section of her long hair with a paper cutter. I am glad it was her hair and not a finger! There are reasons why I am not a doctor, and locating a missing appendage is one of them.

We had an "ugly sweater" contest at school, so I wore the most ostentatious, ridiculous sweater I could find. It had red cardinals, golden snowflakes, gold metal balls, pinecones, and sequins.

To my surprise, several people told me how much they liked my sweater!!

Seriously? Sequins and gold balls? I didn't win the contest.

It reminded me of "Wacky Hair Day" during a previous school year. My hair was pulled up on top of my head in unruly ponytails, and several people complimented me all day about my "cute" hairstyle!

Go figure.

### *Parents Do Not Understand*

The students were asked to provide a written response to the following statement: Parents just don't understand.

Response: "Parents need to stop pretending that they weren't doing the same things when they were teens. I found some pictures, and I saw the 80's hair you thought was so cool.

Oh, and by the way, if those weren't "out past your curfew" boots, then I don't know what they were."

## *Make Him Do His Homework*

After trying without success to contact the father of one of my students, someone finally answered the phone when I called. I introduced myself, explained that I was calling to discuss his son's academic progress, and expressed concern due to some missing assignments.

The man paused briefly, then replied, "Lady, I live in Texas, and I don't even have kids! Day and night, I get calls about Liam not turning in his homework and asking if I can come in for a conference. I DON'T HAVE A KID NAMED LIAM!

Believe me, if I did, I would make him do his homework!"

Apparently the number in our information database was off by one digit.

> Don't tell your kids to grow up just because they're in middle school. If they can't have fun messing around, as adults, they're going to complain that they had a boring childhood.
>
> (even if I'm 30 I'm still going to play video games)

••••••••••••••••••••••••••••••••••

A group of 7th graders created a fictional kingdom called Hipposlumpia in our classroom. The official mascot of Hipposlumpia was a Hipposlump, which was sort of like a winged camel.

The kingdom of Hipposlumpia had official currency, a National Anthem, a holiday, a royal advisor, a mayor, a court jester, royal guards, and several assorted princes and princesses! I had the honor of being the queen!

I'm just curious. Doesn't everyone bring a book to read while they wait for the basketball game to start?

Several people asked me what I was doing, but I thought it was obvious.

After the game, one of my students said, "Ms. Bach, it's Friday night. Put down your book and get a life."

On the first day of Christmas my students gave to me: Brownies. On the second day of Christmas my students gave to me: Fudge. On the third day of Christmas my students gave to me: Cookies.

By the 12th day of Christmas I needed a wheelbarrow!

A student who often neglects to turn in assignments proudly handed me his homework folder. He beamed as I praised him, and he told me he was trying to do better.

Imagine my surprise when I opened the folder later in the afternoon, and found his math homework. I should have attached a bow to it and left it on the math teacher's desk!

We had a fire drill, and when I grabbed the emergency backpack, a large insect came along for the ride. I screamed and threw the backpack down, while trying to get the kids out the door. One of the boys picked up the bug and took it outside. As I picked up the backpack, he said, "The area is secure, ma'am."

For Christmas, a student gave me a paper clip necklace.

I had often wondered what had happened to my paper clips.

CHAPTER 6:

# Would You Like to Repeat That?

*Is that what you meant to say, or would you like to try again? Just like social media posts, once you say something, it's out there.*

As the students were logging into their laptops, one student was trying to figure out how to correct a formatting issue in regard to screen brightness. Another student in the class, attempting to provide assistance, shouted, "Hit the FN key!"

A stunned silence followed, as he continued to repeat, "Hit the FN key! Hit the FN key!"

After a short mini-lesson on the use of the FUNCTION (FN) key, the students were also reminded to think about how others might misinterpret what they are actually trying to say.

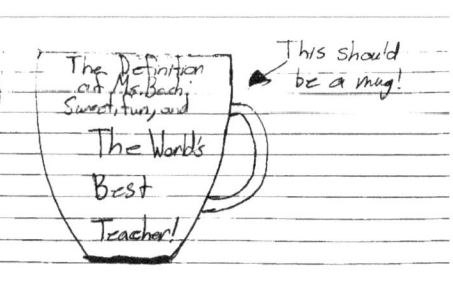

Some students were talking to each other as I was presenting a lesson, so I told them it was my turn to talk.

One student replied, "Again?"

"Happy Thanksgiving, Ms. Bach! I know that many people are thankful for you, including me! Thanks for being you! Hope you had a wonderful Thanksgiving!"

After Open House, I told the students how much I enjoyed having an opportunity to chat with their parents.

One student, who did not attend Open House, asked if I had been able to talk to his dad. "I did talk to your father," I said. "He came in with your baby brother. He is so cute!"

After a pause, the student replied awkwardly, "Uh, Ms. Bach, my dad is married."

I was talking about the baby! The BABY was cute!

For "*Clash Day*" at school, the students wore clothes that didn't match.

Student: "Ms. Bach, this is a great day for you! You don't even need to dress up!"

What? My clothes match most of the time!

"Ms. Bach, you are a great dancer! I don't care what everyone else said."

Really? What did everyone else say?

The students have been studying persuasive debate in regard to a variety of topics. Before they began a class assignment, we discussed the importance of writing a balanced, unbiased essay or article which equally represented both sides of an issue. To get them thinking about a topic they might choose to write about, I asked students to share examples of controversial issues they had seen or read about in the media. One student raised his hand and said that he had seen a group of teachers "streaking" on the news.

Me: "Streaking?"

Student: "Yeah, they were streaking so they would get more money!"

So that is how teachers make more money! I wonder what they wrote on the picket signs.

### *Sex Education*

After concluding their 7th Grade Sex Education class, some of my students were having a disagreement about something they had discussed in class.

One student suggested that they ask me for clarification.

Another student responded, "Ms. Bach? How would she know? She's an English Teacher."

Another student came into my room, eyes glazed over, with a look of disbelief.

"Are you okay?" I asked.

"Ms. Bach, I've decided to adopt children. No way am I ever doing THAT!"

Having trouble getting your middle school students to be quiet? Try this:

Question: "Ms. Bach, what do your cats do all day while you are at school?"

Response: "They take naps and play with their little balls."

Awkward silence.

A student found a new penny on the floor. "Ms. Bach! Look! It's a new penny! Whoa, it has writing on it! I think it's either Mexican or Russian!"

Looking at the penny, I said, "Actually, it's Latin."

His eyes widened and he looked astonished. "Latin pennies? Why do we have Latin pennies? What will the government think of next?"

When the students didn't do a great job in regard to straightening up the room before leaving, I wrote "Describe our exiting procedures" on the board, and asked for written responses.

My favorite: "It was exiting when Ms. Bach brought us treats and played games with us. It was exiting to put up Christmas lights. Oh yeah, and the time Ms. Bach accidentally found a spider."

"Ms. Bach, are we going to read that one book, you know, the one about that guy who goes somewhere and finds that one thing?"

That certainly narrows it down.

The students were having difficulty getting settled down, so I had a conversation with them about the importance of staying focused and giving 100% every day.

I said, "We had moved two steps forward, but now we took five steps back."

One student's response: "Well, at least we made progress!"

I showed the students my 7th grade yearbook. When they saw my picture, one student said, "Ms. Bach, you were cute back then!"

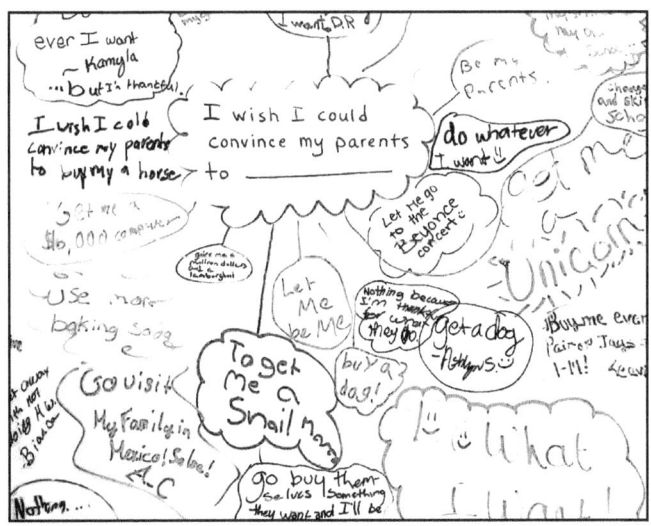

## CHAPTER 7:

# Closing the Generation Gap

*When I was your age…*

"Ms. Bach, have you heard of a band called Journey? They're awesome!"

Me: "Of course I've heard of them. I saw them in concert when I was a teenager."

Student: "Seriously? They have been around that long?"

A large bug crawled up my leg during a lesson.

After witnessing my frantic attempt to extricate the bug from the inside of the leg of my pants, a student said:

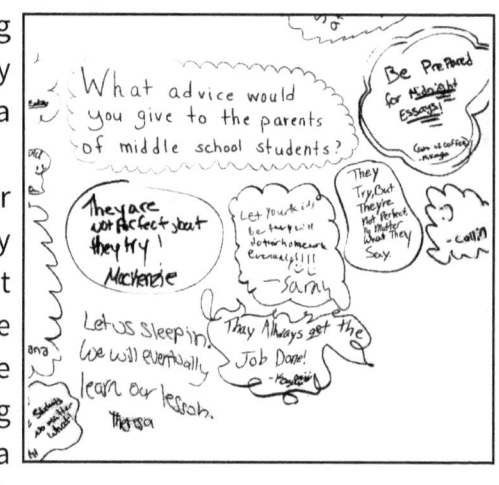

"Wow, Ms. Bach. For someone your age, you can still move like a ninja!"

Excuse me while I attempt to salvage what is left of my dignity.

Student: "Ms. Bach, I don't understand adults. Last night, my mom got mad because I answered her when she asked a question!"

Me: "What was the question?"

Student: "Didn't I tell you not to do that again?"

Me: "What was your response?"

Student: "I told her that she didn't say not to do it again. She said she didn't want to see me do it again. The problem is that she saw me."

After teaching middle school for many years, not much surprises me anymore.

During class, one of my students spontaneously started singing "Eye of the Tiger," which, of course, prompted others to join in. By the time they reached the chorus, several students were not only singing, but dancing as well.

It was their turn to be surprised when, instead of scolding them, I joined in and sang with them.

When the song was over, one student said to another, "See, I told you she would sing with us! She might be old, but she knows that sometimes you just have to let the music out!"

It is true that I believe in setting free the music within us, but since when am I OLD?"

Hey kid, I'll show you old! I still have some moves left.

Me: "I'm staying after school to chaperone the dance."

Student: "I'm glad you will be there, but you aren't actually planning to dance, are you?"

The 7th grade teachers and support staff brought in baby pictures for a contest in which students had to correctly guess who were in the photos.

As two boys looked at the bulletin board, one of them pointed to my picture and remarked, "I think that is Ms. Bach."

The other boy said, "No it isn't, no way is that Ms. Bach."

"Yes it is," the first boy replied, "it has to be Ms. Bach because the picture is so old."

"Ms. Bach, when you were our age, did you have one of those paranoid picture cameras?"

I think I had a Polaroid Camera, but I never had one of the paranoid versions. That must have been a limited edition.

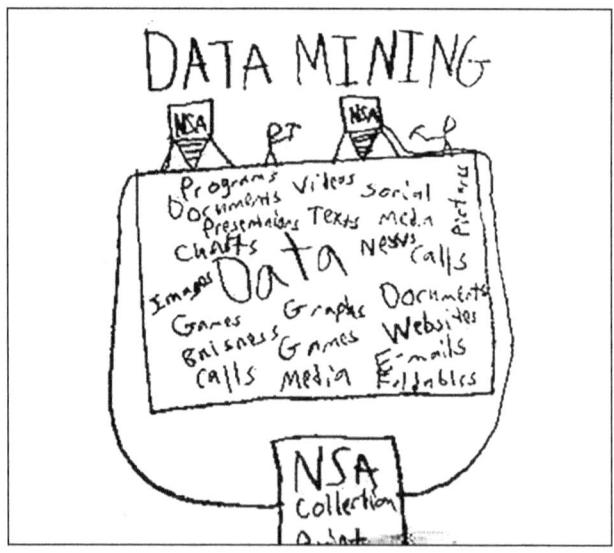

CHAPTER 8:

# Geography Lessons

*Knowing the differences between states, countries, and continents might be important someday, just in case you are supposed to fly to Auckland, but end up in Oakland!*

"Ms. Bach, I wrote a report on the country of Texas!"

Student 1: "I'm moving to Texas."
Student 2: "Which Texas?"

Me: "What will you do this summer?"
Student: "We are going to South Virginia. I think it's somewhere in New York."

As I was sharing stories about my recent trip to Europe with the students, I told them about my flight being delayed due to a snowstorm in Europe, and how it caused me to miss my former foreign-exchange student's graduation from medical school.
One student had an excellent solution to the problem: "Why didn't you just drive?"

One of my students informed me that it was his last day, since he and his family were moving to Anchorage, Alaska. When I asked him if they would be driving he replied, "Of course not, Ms. Bach! We have to fly because Alaska is an island!"

Oh, of course! How silly of me! I thought he might be moving to the Alaska that is attached to Canada.

A student told me that his mom recently gave birth to a baby.

When I asked how many children were now in his family, he told me that there were three: the baby, himself, and a 5th grader.

He said, "My dad told me that she wanted another baby because her geological clock was ticking."

CHAPTER 9:
# Rogue Reading

*If you want to know what your middle school child is thinking, ask them to interpret the plot elements of a fairy tale. Maybe there are some things you shouldn't know.*

Question: What was the primary conflict in the Cinderella story?
Response: "Cinderella needed to kick her stepmother's butt, and get the hell out!"

Question: What did Cinderella leave behind when she left the ball?
Student 1: Cinderella left behind a glass stripper.
Student 2: Cinderella left behind a grass sniper.

Question: In the story of Cinderella, what is the prince's problem?
Response: "The prince's problem is that he shouldn't go chasing after girls in the first place. Girls are trouble because of all their drama, and he will just get distracted. Also, with girls, why is it always about shoes?"

The students were asked to write a summary of the story we had just finished reading. When one student repeatedly said he couldn't remember any details from the story, I suggested that he might want to get a book and review the text. He walked across the room and returned to his desk with a dictionary. No wonder he couldn't remember any details from the story.

A dictionary?

Student: "Are we going to be reading Oliver Twit this year?"

Student: "The setting of the story takes place in Cheesecake Bay."
I think he meant Chesapeake Bay. It could be fun to live in Cheesecake Bay!

We read *The Veldt* by Ray Bradbury, in which a family lived in a futuristic home that was completely automated. The children's bedroom could be transformed into any realistic scene, based on the child's thoughts.

I asked the students to describe a scene they would create if such a bedroom existed.

One student wrote: "I would have a swimming pool, with seventy-five people wearing penguin suits who would be catapulted into the pool."

CHAPTER 10:

# Back to the Beginning

*Have you ever been driving in circles while lost before ending up back where you started? As band leaders say, "Let's take it from the top!"*

Parts of Speech Review: What is a conjunction?
Student A: "A conjunction is when you put an apostrophe in a word like can't."
Student B: "That's a contraction!"
Student A: "No it isn't, a contraction is what happens when someone has a baby."
Student B: "Sometimes words have more than one meaning, you know."
Student A: "So what's a conjunction then?"
I'm pretty sure that was my original question.

Student A: "I wrote about an organelle."
Student B: "You mean one of those piano things at church with all the pipes?"
Student A: "No, that's an organ."
Student C: "I've been to Oregon!"
Another five-star middle school conversation.

Me: "Look at the plot line and tell me what happened during the climax of the story."
Student: "It's when the story talked about the weather."
Me: "Are you talking about climate?"
Student: "Yeah, what are you talking about?"

## *Questions Questions Questions ???*

After spending three days identifying, discussing, and writing about text features, I asked the students to locate text features in a magazine, and explain how they are helpful and useful to readers.
Questions? "Ms. Bach, what is a text feature?"

Question: In what ways can word choice impact the effectiveness of our writing? How can we energize our writing by using vivid, interesting vocabulary?
Response: "We need to use higher vocabulary instead of lower vocabulary because we won't learn new vocabulary unless we learn higher vocabulary."

The students were asked to write about their academic strengths and weaknesses, and provide specific examples of ways in which they excelled or struggled in regard to school.
Student Response: "I don't like math, because word problems confuse me and I can never figure out what X is supposed to be. I don't do good in math, but my mom says that I should do good in math because I have my dad's jeans. Since we can only wear jeans on Fridays, I guess I will do good on Fridays. I don't get how getting somebody's jeans can help you do good, but I hope it works."

"Ms. Bach, how old were you when you were my age?"

Student: "Ms. Bach, doesn't that word have one of those up in the air commas?"
Me: "An apostrophe?"
Student: "Yeah, you know, those things that go in a conjunction."
Me: "Don't you mean a contraction?"
Student: "Ms. Bach, you're confusing me."
Buddy, I think you were confused before we started this conversation.

Me: "Who wrote The Diary of Anne Frank?"
Student: "How would I know? I haven't read it yet!"

Me: "Why are you sitting all by yourself?"
Student: "Ms. Bach, sometimes I just need a fortress of solitude."

Question: What did you do during the break?
Response: "I rode a four-wheeler and didn't die. After that, I traveled to my couch, where I played Minecraft until 2:00 AM."

Question: What is your favorite candy?
Answer: "Sweat Tarts"

Question: What is the difference between a noun and a pronoun?
Response: "A pronoun is a noun that has some mad skills."

Question: What is the title of your personal narrative?
Response: "The Day My Mom Got Pregnant"

Question: As your teacher, what might be something important I should know about you?
Response: "Well, since coming to your class, I have been completely normal."

Question: What does the word valor mean?
Student #1: "Isn't it a car?"
Student #2: "No, it isn't a car. It's the guy who parks the cars!"

Question: If you could write a poem about anything, what would you write about?
Response: "If I could write a poem about anything, I would write about chipmunks, because they are the scariest creatures on the earth.
When you are bitten by a chipmunk, you bleed profusely."
That's good to know. You don't just bleed, you bleed profusely! Apparently, SOMEONE listened during the lesson about adverbs.

Question: What is a reflexive pronoun?
Response: "A reflexive pronoun is a pronoun that reacts to something like a ninja."

	Question: How tall are you?
	Response: "I'm five foot twelve."

Chapter 12

# Crossing the Line

*Misspelled or out of context words can lead to embarrassing written responses. Should this chapter be labeled PG-13?*

Students were asked to write about a problem or conflict they have encountered at school and possible solutions that might resolve the issue. Response: "We have bulls at our school. They are mean and I do not lick them. If no one licks them, maybe they will go away."

Did he mean "bullies?" I hope there are no bulls running around school! I agree that licking them would be a bad idea.

Response: "One reason why our school should have uniforms is because some days students come to school half-naked. You should only be naked in the shower, or when your clothes are in the dryer."

"We got my dad a new girl for Father's Day, because they were on sale at Home Depot."

All he asked for was a grill, but he apparently got a new girl instead!

My students wrote fictional narratives, and were asked to trade papers with a partner, and provide a written response in regard to the other person's story.

One student's response: "I licked your story. I hope you licked mine."

Question: Should kids spend more time in school?
Response: "Kids are already smarter than adults. We know whazzup. And if the teacher gets too tired she might turn into a beach."
A beach? Yeah, I know whazzup.

Imaginative Writing: "On a Thursday afternoon I went to go find my band instrument in the closet. There was a hoe on the floor of my closet that I didn't notice before, but it was as big as a tuba. Inside the hoe was a time machine. You never know what you might find in a closet."

I asked my students to write about a memorable day from the previous school year. One student wrote, "Last year, the lust day at school was memorable to me. We had a party!"

I can imagine how the "lust" day might have been memorable! Inappropriate, but definitely memorable.

**Instructions:
Find a text
feature in the brochure.
Response: "I found a
diaphragm in the brochure."**

The students were asked to write about something they know how to do well, and explain the steps taken to become successful at their endeavor. One student wrote: "I am really good at celebrity impregnations. I am good at this because I practice a lot!"

A student brought me a wrapped gift for Teacher Appreciation Week. As I was opening it, he told me that he saw a book at a yard sale, and since he knew I loved books, he bought it for me.

Instead of a novel or book of poetry, imagine my surprise when I opened it and saw the title that read: *What's Happening to My Body? A Book for Boys.*

As I stared at the book, wondering what to say, he excitedly asked, "Can you believe that this book only cost $1.50?"

I flipped through some of the pages, noticing that in addition to some interesting and thought-provoking chapter topics, there were diagrams and illustrations as well. An added bonus!

Uh, thanks, I think? If any of you have a pre-teen boy, and need to "have the talk" with him, I have a book for you!

> **"When our house was bummed we called the State Farmers to help cuz they got your back."**

After a class debate about the school's dress code, I asked the students to write one opinion statement about the subject.

One student wrote: "Having a dress code is unfair because I don't like to tuck in my shit!"

The misspelling the word "shirt" reminded me of a time when I used to teach a drama class. I sent a letter to thirty parents, informing them that if they wanted to purchase a T-shirt or sweatshirt for our theater production, order forms were available. Inadvertently, I left out the "r" in the word "sweatshirt."

Hey parents and students, "Would you like to order a sweatshit?"

Question: What is something that you don't like about school? Response: "Ms. Bach, I hate workshits!"

Dear Ms. Bach,
I had a great year in your class! You're pretty awesome for someone your age. Since you are like my school mom, I think you should take me to Disney World this summer. Come on, you know you want to! I'll miss you next year.
Love,
Kristina

Dear Ms. Bach,
I'm sorry I didn't turn in my homework. I got home late because I had to go shopping with my dad. We had to buy a three piece slut.
Bryan

The students had been studying poetry, and after analyzing a poem in class, they had an opportunity to practice writing a free verse poem on a topic of their choice. Heard from across the room: "Ms. Bach, how do you spell sex?"

Of course, he instantly had the attention of all the other kids. I was thinking that maybe he had been watching too much late-night cable television.

Then he clarified his request: "I already have the first two letters, I and N." Writing poetry about bugs is a bit less awkward in middle school.

While analyzing a poem, the students were identifying literary elements within the text. When asked to identify the poem's protagonist, one student responded that the protagonist is the "ho."

I'm sure he meant to say hero.

### "I turned on the ho's for my dad after he mowed the lawn."

After watching How the Grinch Stole Christmas the students were asked to describe the main character, and explain how the events in the story caused him to change from the beginning of the story to the end.

Student response: "The Grinch was a badass, and all he wanted to do was go to Ho Ville and get everything he wanted."

We were discussing different forms of writing, and I asked the students to think of various writing features found in newspapers. One student's response: "I think there is an advice feature in the newspaper where people write letters to Abigail Van Urine."

CHAPTER 13:

# Dear Ms. Bach

*Among my greatest treasures are notes, cards, and letters from students. Every message, heartwarming or hilarious, will be cherished until the end of my days. I am thankful for students, past and present, who took the time to write to me.*

**On a Valentine's Day card:**

Dear Ms. Bach,

I am giving you a card for Valentine's Day, because I didn't think anyone else would give you one. It's not like you have a boyfriend or anything. Anyway, I hope you aren't lonely. Thanks for making cookies for us. I am glad you don't have a boyfriend, because then he would probably eat all of them. You're a great teacher. Happy Valentine's Day.

From, Nick

Dear Ms. Bach,
Thank you for bringing us poopsicles on Fridays. You're almost as nice as my mom.
Sincerely,
Grace

**Note found on my desk:**

Dear Ms. Bach,

I am raising money for my Boy Scout Troop and was wondering if you had any poop cans to donate.

Thank you,
Jack

Dear Ms. Bach,

I just wanted to say thank you for all of your support. I love that you can teach and be caring at the same time. You support the fact that I wish to be a SEAL and I appreciate that. Thank you. I'm on SEAL Team Bach, and I'm not ringing the bell. I hope you will come to my SEAL Team graduation someday.

Sincerely,
Aaron

Dear Ms. Bach,

I wanted you to know that I like your class. When I found out you would be my teacher I was happy, because some of your students from last year told me that you are awesome! Everything they said about you is true. Well, almost everything. Anyway, I hope you are having a good day.

Love,
Reagan
PS: Don't tell anyone, but I still like Hannah Montana.

I am so happy to have you as a teacher! You always have a joke to tell, and you are always full of laughter and joy.

Thank you!

Dear Ms. Bach,
I am so thankful I was a part of your class. I am going to miss you so much! You have been a good influence in my life. I would like to give a shout out to your amazing mom, and God, of course, and your dad for raising such a wonderful and generous woman. I can't imagine what I would be doing if I didn't have you for a teacher. I love you.
Sincerely,
Brittany

Dear Ms. Bach,
I talked it over with my friends and we have decided to like you. We promise not to give you any trouble this year. Have a nice day!


A student who was very quiet left a note on my desk:
Dear Ms. Bach,
My mom said that I should make a New Year Resolution to work on being more social, since I don't usually talk to people. She said I should talk to people about myself and tell them things about me. Ms. Bach, I like fudge. I hope my mom is happy now.
Sincerely,
Hannah

Dear Ms. Bach,

When we had our Poetry Slam you read a poem about your dad and how much he liked motorcycles, so I made a motorcycle out of paperclips for you. I hope it reminds you of your dad.

Sincerely,
Billy

> I have 7 amazing teachers. I love each and everyone of them. They all teach and tell me different things. My favorit class of the day is First period, because we get to do Friday free writes and my Favorit teacher is in First period. She comes to support almost all my volleyball games. and she is very funny and nice. She also teaches very well, and makes Things clear. I Love My first Period Teacher, Mrs. Bach!!

Dear Ms. Bach,

I am sorry to tell you I didn't do my homework. We had a very busy weekend. My parents had a lot to do, so I had to do chores while they went shopping and worked on getting me a baby brother. I will finish the homework tonight.

Sincerely,
Elliott

Dear Ms. Bach,

I hope you had a good Thanksgiving. I missed you, so I brought you three marshmallows. If you don't eat them, maybe you could put them together with toothpicks to make a snowman. Have a great day!

Sincerely,

Robert

Dear Ms. Bach,

How are you? I hope you had a good weekend. Did you do anything fun like go to a birthday party? I was thinking about what you said last Thursday on 9-11, about making sure we tell people how much we love them, and say thank you, because we don't know what will happen, and we don't want to wait until it is too late. I wanted to tell you that I am thankful to be in your class. You really care about us. When you said you would give your life to protect us, I really thought about that, so some of us prayed for you this weekend.

Thank you, Ms. Bach.

Love,

Danielle

PS: Your new shoes are the bomb. I have Converse too, but mine are red.

Dear Ms. Bach,

I had a great year in your class! You're pretty awesome for someone your age. Since you are like my school mom, I think you should take me to Disney World this summer. Come on, you know you want to! I'll miss you next year.

Love,
Kristina

## *From A Parent*

Dear Ms. Bach,

I just wanted to say thank you! Thank you for being an amazing teacher, friend, and listener! Thank you for being an inspiration to my children and thank you for believing in them when others may not! Thank you for supporting them and paving the future for them! Thank you for always pointing out the positive even when things seem so very negative! You are a change agent! You are a true mentor! Thousands of children are blessed to have you in their lives and to benefit from your spirit! I am thankful mine are among those!

Sincerely,
Mrs. Green

> I miss you! I miss all the games we played and Free-Write Fridays. You have given me much more confidence in my writing. I still have some of the poems I wrote. I also remember the Jabberwocky poem word for word. I can't wait to read your new book. I hope you and your cats have made a good transition into your new house. Hopefully it has a big kitchen were you can make a lot of cookies!
>
> Sincerely,

## Thanks Mrs. Bach 4-14-12

Mrs. Bach I just wanted to take my time and say thank you for everything. No teacher has given me snacks or any treat but you did. I also wanted to say thank you for putting up with me all year. I've been telling my parents that you're most likely to be my favorite teacher in the 7th grade. So, I just wanted to say thank you for everything you've done for me and all the other students on this team. I also wanted to thank you for all those funny moments you give us. This year and this class will be one thing I will never forget. So, thank you for all the wonderful 7th grade memories I get to keep for ever and ever.

Dear Ms Bach,

I can't begin to tell you how grateful I am to have had you as my teacher this year. Not only did we have tons of fun during the school year, but you were kind and caring to all of your students. There are a lot of teachers who have lost their passion for teaching. You, Ms Bach, have not. You love your job and you genuinely care about your students. I would just like to say thank you for caring about me, and showing me how much potential I have. I have always had a passion for writing, and you have made my love for it grow in unimaginable ways. I really will miss the Friday Free-writes, though. I even do it at home now, jotting down my thoughts and feelings. I've always been a shy girl, but your class gave me the opportunity to befriend two amazing friends. I would like to say thank you for that as well. Even though this year was definitley far from perfect, I am still very glad that I have met you, and attended your class. If ever I am to be successful one day, I will come back to find you, and give you anything I can. Thank you, Ms. Bach.

You've always been one of my favorite teachers. If I could next year, I'd go to your class again in a heartbeat. I'm glad you've been one of my teachers this year. (By the way, I'm working on a book of short stories that I plan to publish). I'm glad to have been one of your students this year.

Thank you for saying that I belong in this world, also that I have a purpose, because, before, I didn't believe I had anything to live for... Anyway, I'm flattered and feel special that if you had a daughter, that you'd want one like me. 😊 Thank you for being my most favorite teacher, and I appreciate the life-lessons you teach us. 😊 I hope you have an amazing day! And

---

I made it through the year with some great memories. My best memorie in this class is when we did camp fire stories. I love at the end of this class we always have free time and talk to you about anything whether it's Starbucks, cheer, or how our day went. You were the best teacher by far. Ms. Bach has taught me so much with my writing skills and she has grown me up through the year. She is always silly and makes these long speeches that can change my perspective on a lot of things. I hope that next year I can see Ms. Bach again and we can all get a second period re-union and eat cookies. Ms. Bach is so supporting with the basketball games, and teaching students new things every day. Best year ever!

MIDDLE SCHOOL UPDATE

LORRI BACH

www.ingramcontent.com/pod-product-compliance
Lightning Source LLC
Chambersburg PA
CBHW071222070526
44584CB00019B/3115